LAW CARTOONS

AUSTRALIA
The Law Book Company
Brisbane • Sydney • Melbourne • Perth

CANADA
Carswell
Ottawa • Toronto • Calgary • Montreal • Vancouver

AGENTS
Steimatzky's Agency Ltd., Tel Aviv;
N.M. Tripathi (Private) Ltd., Bombay;
Eastern Law House (Private) Ltd., Calcutta;
M.P.P. House, Bangalore;
Universal Book Traders, Delhi;
Aditya Books, Delhi;
MacMillan Shuppan KK, Tokyo;
Pakistan Law House, Karachi, Lahore

LAW CARTOONS

by

Susan Tayfoor, LL.B.

Lecturer, Birkbeck College

First Edition

LONDON
SWEET & MAXWELL
1995

Published in 1995 by
Sweet & Maxwell Limited
of South Quay Plaza,
183 Marsh Wall, London E14 9FT

Printed in Great Britain by The Headway Press Ltd.

A CIP catalogue record for this book
is available from the British Library

ISBN 0-421-544600

No natural forests were destroyed to make this product only farmed timber
was used and re-planted.

CONTENTS

GLOSSARY OF SOME LEGAL TERMS

CONDITION A condition is an important term of a contract, breach of which gives the innocent party the right to treat the contract as cancelled

CONSIDERATION Is something of value given or done in return for the other party's promise, eg. someone gives you a book and you give £5 in return. The £5 is your consideration.

CONTRA PREFERENTUM Where a document is ambiguous, the least favourable interpretation of it will be applied against the person who wrote it, or is relying on it.

DURESS To make a contract under duress means to be forced into a contract, for example, by threats of unlawful violence.

INJUNCTION A court order which restrains a person from doing a particular thing.

INVITATION TO TREAT This is not an offer, but an expression of someone's willingness to enter into negotiations, eg. a display of goods in a shop window with a price tag.

NON EST FACTUM 'Not his deed' - This is a plea used to show you signed a document by mistake. If the plea is successful, the contract will be void

PROMISSORY ESTOPPEL Estoppel is to prevent someone from denying the truth of what they previously said, and going back on a promise.

QUANTUM MERUIT	'As much as he has earned'. For example, if someone completes one third of the work under a contract, they may be able to claim one third of payment owing, on a quantum meruit basis.
RESCISSION	Is an equitable remedy which has the effect of cancelling the contract, and putting the parties back to their original positions.
RECTIFICATION	Is the court's correction of a mistake made by both parties in drawing up a contract.
SPECIFIC PERFORMANCE	Is an equitable remedy where the court will order a person to do what they've agreed to do under the contract
UBERRIMAE FIDEI	'Of the utmost faith'. A contract is uberrimae fidei where the person making it is under a duty to disclose all relevant information.
VOID CONTRACTS	A void contract has no legal effect, and property cannot usually be passed under a void contract.
VOIDABLE CONTRACTS	A voidable contract is valid until one party decides to rescind (cancel) it. If the property has passed to a third party in the meantime, they will get good title (ownership)
WAIVER	To waive your rights is to give up a right you have in law, for example, the right to sue someone on a promise they made.

CHAPTER ONE - OFFER AND ACCEPTANCE

offeror
(person making the offer)

offeree
(person to whom the offer is made)
the acceptor once the offer is accepted

> An offer is an expression of willingness to contract on certain terms, made with the intention that it shall become binding as soon as it is accepted by the person to whom it is addressed
>
> G. H. Treitel

Once accepted, therefore, this will usually result in a binding contract, which neither side can freely back out of

An offer can be made to one person...

You can have it for £50.

£50 reward for return of lost cat

...or to the world at large

This type of offer, in return for doing an act, is accepted as soon as someone carries out the act, and will result in a UNILATERAL CONTRACT.

One famous example of a unilateral contract is found in the case…

Carlill v. Carbolic Smoke Ball Co. 1893

13th Nov. 1891

Pall Mall Gazette
ADVERT
Our smoke balls protect you from influenza. If you catch influenza after using them, we will pay you £100

INFLUENZA EPIDEMIC! THOUSANDS DEAD!

I used the smoke balls, and caught influenza, and now I want the £100 you promised

Ahem… It wasn't an offer you were supposed to take seriously. Anyway, we didn't know you'd accepted the offer.

It was held that the offer was accepted when the plaintiff used the smokeballs as requested. This resulted in a unilateral contract, where there was no need to notify the company of her acceptance - doing the act was enough.
The smokeball company was ordered to pay the plaintiff £100 as promised.

RED MINI FOR SALE - £500

What happens if 100 people answer my advert? Do I have a binding contract with 100 people?

No, because not everything which looks like an offer will be interpreted as one. Advertisments in newspapers, or price tags on goods, will usually be regarded as an
INVITATION TO TREAT

What's the difference between an offer, and an invitation to treat?

  £20 Daily News Car for sale £60

↑ ↑
invitations to treat

An invitation to treat is when you invite the other person to make you an offer, which you are then free to accept or refuse.

<u>Displaying goods in a shop window or shelf</u>

Stitch+Blade
Flickknives 10s
<u>Fisher v. Bell 1961</u>

This will not be an offer, but an invitation to treat. The shopkeeper is expressing his willingness to contract with a customer. The contract is made not when the customer hands over the money, but when the shopkeeper accepts it.

<u>Adverts in a newspaper</u>

Bramblefinchhens 60s each
<u>Partridge v. Crittenden 1968</u>

An advert for goods will usually be considered an invitation to treat. In this case, the offer is made when you reply to the advert, and acceptance takes place when the offeror sends the goods.

When does an offer terminate?

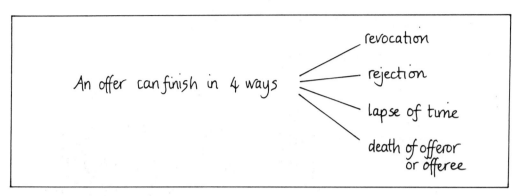

An offer can finish in 4 ways
- revocation
- rejection
- lapse of time
- death of offeror or offeree

---

① <u>Revocation</u>

I've changed my mind, the offer's closed.

The offer can be taken back at any point before it's accepted, but the offeree must know of the revocation.

It's a letter saying their offer's no longer open, but I've just written accepting it

<u>Henthorn v. Fraser 1892</u>

The revocation arrived too late to be effective. There was already a binding contract.

The offeree must hear about the revocation either directly from the person who made the offer, or from a reliable source of information.

This could also be through a mutual friend.

<u>Dickinson v. Dodds 1876</u>

4

② <u>Rejection</u>

or counter offer

③ <u>Lapse of Time</u>

If the offer doesn't state how long it will remain open for, it will finish after a reasonable length of time

You know that car you offered me last year - I've decided to take it

The offer will have expired.

What is a reasonable length of time can vary from a matter of hours, or a few months, depending on what is being offered, and how the offer is made (eg. fax, post)

④ <u>Death</u>

Of the offeror or offeree can terminate the offer, especially if it is an offer involving a 'personal' service, such as teaching.

Acceptance

Acceptance can be by words or conduct, but it must be on exactly the same terms as the offer

A: Will you buy my car for £600?

B: I'll give you £300 now, and the rest in instalments.

↑ counter offer

By changing the terms of the offer, B has made a counter-offer, which it's up to A to accept or reject

Once a counter offer is made, the original offer is finished, and can no longer be accepted

Does acceptance have to be communicated to the offeror?

———— Usually, yes ————

Dear Nephew,
    This is an offer to buy your horse for £30. If I hear no more about it, I shall consider the horse mine.
    Uncle

The nephew didn't reply, and the question arose as to whether there was a contract between the uncle and the nephew.

Unless there are exceptional circumstances, silence cannot be presumed to equal acceptance

Felthouse v. Bindley 1862

How must acceptance be communicated?

Usually, the acceptance must be heard / received to be effective...

Until A repeats her acceptance there is no binding contract (Entores Ltd v. Miles Far East Corporation 1955

This applies, when the contract is made by instantaneous means, e.g. acceptance by fax, telephone, telex, face-to-face...

However, there is something called the POSTAL RULE

Denning L.J.

When a contract is made by post, it is clear law... that the acceptance is complete as soon as the letter is put into the post box, and that is the place where the contract is made

So if it is reasonable to reply to an offer by post, there will be a binding contract as soon as the letter is properly stamped, addressed and posted. Even if it never arrives!

I don't want to be bound by a letter of acceptance I never received!

offeror

By including the words 'notice in writing' (or similar words), the offeror sets aside the postal rule, and the acceptance must be received for a contract to exist.

Holwell Securities v. Hughes

QUIZ - OFFER AND ACCEPTANCE

① You return someone's cat, and later see there was a
£50 reward offered for this. Can you go back and claim it?

Yes / No ?

② Acceptance must always be communicated.

Yes / No ?

③ You offer to sell your car to someone, and promise them you'll
keep the offer open for 1 week. Can you sell it to someone
else the next day?

Yes / No ?

④ You hand a letter of acceptance to a postman delivering
letters. If it gets lost, is there a binding contract?

Yes / No ?

⑤ John offers his car to Noel for £500. Noel asks 'Would you
take £450?" John shakes his head, and Noel agrees to the
original price of £500. John cannot refuse to sell it to
him, since the offer has been accepted.

True / False ?

⑥ If the offer says "reply by first class post", and you
accept by fax, there isn't a valid acceptance, since
it wasn't made in the proper way.

True / False ?

8

CHAPTER TWO - CONSIDERATION

B hasn't agreed to do anything in return for A's promise. B has provided no consideration for A's promise, so there is no binding contract

 So, what is consideration? It's what you do, as your part of the bargain.

In the words of Lord Devlin...

An act or forbearance of one party, or the promise thereof, is the price for which the promise of the other is bought, and the promise thus given for value is enforceable

for example, consideration can be — the money you give for the book you buy

a service in return for money, eg. washing windows

Types of Consideration

Executory — I'll pay you when you deliver the goods ...Both sides still have to carry out their promises, and the consideration is 'executory' - still to be done

Executed — I've paid you, now deliver the goods — A has fulfilled his part of the promise, so A's consideration is 'executed' - carried out.

Consideration can be nominal

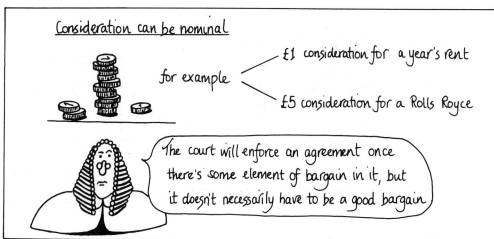

for example

£1 consideration for a year's rent

£5 consideration for a Rolls Royce

The court will enforce an agreement once there's some element of bargain in it, but it doesn't necessarily have to be a good bargain

Consideration can also be a promise NOT to do something

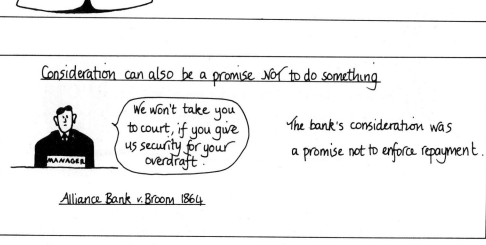

MANAGER

We won't take you to court, if you give us security for your overdraft.

The bank's consideration was a promise not to enforce repayment.

Alliance Bank v. Broom 1864

However, it must have some economic value

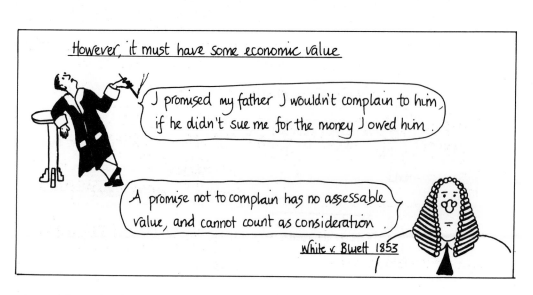

I promised my father I wouldn't complain to him, if he didn't sue me for the money I owed him.

A promise not to complain has no assessable value, and cannot count as consideration.

White v. Bluett 1853

<u>Past Consideration will not be binding</u>

B's act was completed before A offered the £50, not in return for the promise.

B cannot enforce A's promise to pay £10, since B's consideration is past.

This rule can be seen in the case <u>Re McArdle 1951</u>

A widow made a number of improvements on a house which had been left to her children.

Some time later, they signed a document

> Dear Mum,
> We promise to pay you £488 for the work you did on the house.

They later refused to pay, and she tried to enforce the payment

Since she'd already done the work before the children mentioned payment, her consideration was past, and the promise to pay was unenforceable.

One of the exceptions to this rule, however, is when the act is done at the promisor's request, and both parties assume payment would be made for the act.

The promise to pay was enforceable, even though the pardon was obtained before the promise was given.

11

Is a promise to pay extra enforceable?

If you agree to pay someone £100 for a task, then halfway through the task you promise to pay double that amount, is your promise enforceable?

The traditional view was found in a case in 1809...

Two crew members deserted a ship, in a foreign port

If you get the ship home, I'll pay you all extra, and share the deserters' wages amongst you

Once home, the captain refused to pay the extra wages, and the court held that the promise was unenforceable.

The crew were only carrying out an existing duty, they'd already agreed to do. By doing the same duty, they provided no consideration for the captain's promise to pay extra money

Stilk v. Myrick 1809

This rule was qualified, however, in a recent case...

If someone freely makes a promise to pay extra money, and both parties derive some sort of benefit from the contract, the promise will be enforceable.

Williams v. Roffey Bros & Nicholls (Contractors) Ltd 1991

The Doctrine of Waiver

 If someone owes me money, and I agree to accept half, in full payment, can I then change my mind and insist on the rest?

Under the common law rule you could. Even though you'd agreed to 'waive' your rights, you could always go back on your promise and insist they pay you the rest of the money.

This is called the rule in Pinnel's Case

However, this rule was recognised as unfair, and the courts developed the doctrine of promissory estoppel, to stop someone from going back on their promise...

Lord Denning

 In my opinion... the promise to accept a smaller sum in discharge of a larger sum, if acted upon, is binding.

Central London Property Trust Ltd v. High Trees House Ltd. 1947

QUIZ - CONSIDERATION

① You promise to give someone £50 for the lecture notes you borrowed last year. Is your promise enforceable?

Yes / No ?

② "I will give you £50, if you will come to my house" Have both parties given consideration?

Yes / No ?

③ You lose your job, and your landlord agrees to lower your rent until you find a new one. However long you take, your landlord cannot go back on his promise.

True / False ?

④ A promises to pay you £100 if B promises to do the same. If one of them doesn't pay you, can you enforce their promise?

Yes / No ?

⑤ You promise to pay someone in one year's time, if they deliver goods to you now. When the time comes to pay them, you can argue that their consideration is past

True / False ?

⑥ A 'bare promise' is never enforceable.

True / False ?

CHAPTER THREE · INTENTION TO CREATE LEGAL RELATIONS

For an agreement to be enforceable in court, the parties must intend it to be legally binding

Obviously in a case like this, neither person intends to take the other to court, if they don't keep the agreement. There is no intention to create legal relations

When will an agreement not be legally binding?

If the person didn't mean anyone to take his words seriously...

£100 to the man who'll marry my daughter!

Weeks v. Tybald 1605

These words were held to be mere 'puff', and not intended to be taken seriously.

If the parties expressly state this intention in writing

This agreement is not legally binding

(Commercial agreements are presumed to be legally binding, unless the parties expressly state otherwise)

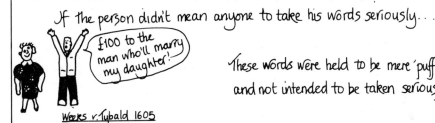

Social arrangements are not legally enforceable, such as

- inviting a guest to dinner,
- offering someone a lift
- a promise to play golf

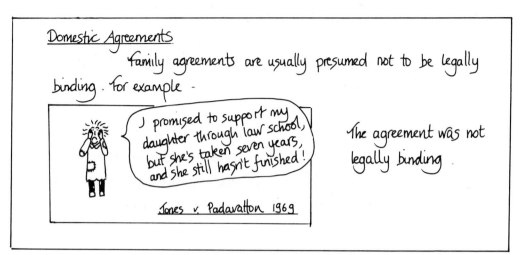

Domestic Agreements

Family agreements are usually presumed not to be legally binding. For example -

I promised to support my daughter through law school, but she's taken seven years, and she still hasn't finished!

Jones v. Padavatton 1969

The agreement was not legally binding.

Agreements between spouses are not usually binding

My husband promised to pay me £30 a month while he was abroad.

But I didn't expect her to sue me if I didn't!

Atkin LJ →

The common law does not regulate... agreements between spouses. Their promises are not sealed with seals and sealing wax.

Balfour v Balfour 1919

However, if the husband and wife were about to separate, the decision would be different, and any agreements they make then would probably be enforced by the courts.

QUIZ - INTENTION TO CREATE LEGAL RELATIONS

① You promise your friend that if she pays for dinner today, you'll pay for it tomorrow. The next day you refuse to pay. Was your promise enforceable?

Yes / No ?

② You agree to go shares with three other people on a lottery ticket. It's a winning ticket, but they refuse to share the money. Is the agreement enforceable?

Yes / No ?

③ If, on the lottery ticket it states "binding in honour only" there is no legal obligation for them to pay out any prize money.

True / False ?

④ "If you come and marry me, I promise to leave you my house" - This type of promise can never be legally binding.

True / False ?

⑤ If a husband and wife set up a business together, the agreement will be presumed to be legally binding, even though it is between a husband and wife.

True / False ?

CHAPTER FOUR   - CAPACITY TO CONTRACT

Not everyone has full capacity to contract — Minors
Restrictions apply as to the types of — drunks
contracts made for example by — the mentally ill

The resulting contract may be...

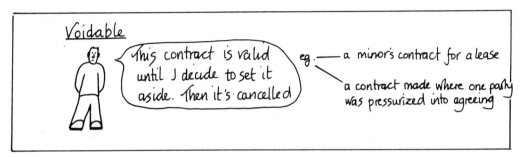

Voidable

This contract is valid until J decide to set it aside. Then it's cancelled

e.g. — a minor's contract for a lease

a contract made where one party was pressurized into agreeing

Unenforceable

If I don't want to do my part of the contract, the other party can't force me to do it.

e.g. — a contract with a minor to pay for luxury goods

a bare promise to give money to someone

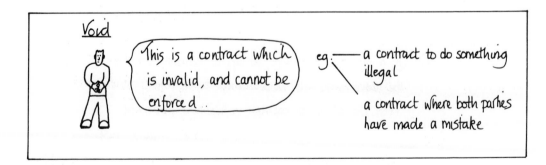

Void

This is a contract which is invalid, and cannot be enforced ..

e.g. — a contract to do something illegal

a contract where both parties have made a mistake

← under 18

Minors' Contracts

A minor does not have full capacity to contract, and minors' contracts can be divided into 3 types...

— Valid (e.g. contracts for necessary goods)

— Voidable (e.g. contracts for a lease)

— Unenforceable (e.g. contracts for luxury goods)

An important act concerning minors' contracts is the

MINORS' CONTRACTS ACT 1987

 This states that if J order goods, then refuse to pay when they are delivered, the court will only enforce payment (of a reasonable price) only if they are necessaries.

Shopkeeper → But what exactly are necessaries?

"Necessaries" means goods suitable to the condition in life of the minor... and to his actual requirements at the time of sale or delivery (s. 3)

Sale of Goods Act 1979

for example...  one overcoat, please

 Twenty Armani jackets please

Binding - it's reasonable to consider an overcoat a necessity

Unenforceable - it would be impossible to argue he needed twenty jackets

What is necessary also depends on the minor's 'station in life'

Nash v. Inman 1908

The tailor had to prove two points:
① Eleven waistcoats were suitable for the minor's way of life
    and also
② That he was not already supplied with enough waistcoats.

What happens if the minor is given non-necessary goods?

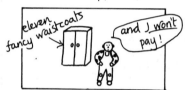

The court can order restitution (s.3 Minor's Contracts Act 1987)

or, if the minor sells the goods, the courts can reclaim the money, if the funds are identifiable (e.g. the money was kept separately)

Service Contracts

To be enforceable, a contract of employment must be for the minor's benefit

Employer

CONDITIONS OF EMPLOYMENT
① The employer can break the contract, if the girl is no good

② The girl must work for no one else

③ The employer needn't provide work for her.

Stage Dancer

The contract was unenforceable since it wasn't for the minor's benefit
De Frantesco v. Barnum 1890

Contracts by the mentally ill

For Non-Necessaries:

Were you so ill at the time you made the contract, that you didn't know what you were doing?

Yes

The contract will be voidable as long as the other person had no way of knowing of their mental illness.

For Necessaries:

If the goods were suitable for your position in life, you must pay for them.

Contracts by drunken persons

For Non-Necessaries:

Were you so drunk that at the time you made the contract, you didn't know what you were doing?

hic!

The contract will be voidable at the drunk person's option, as long as the other person realised they were intoxicated.

So when I sober up, I can accept it, or cancel it.

For Necessaries:

Contracts for necessaries are binding in the same way as for minors.

QUIZ - CAPACITY TO CONTRACT

① A minor buys a multi-gym machine, changes his mind, and wants to return it. He will be able to do so, since it comes under luxury goods.

True / False ?

② If a shopkeeper delivers necessary goods to a minor, he will be able to get full payment for them.

True / False ?

③ A minor takes a gold necklace on credit, and exchanges it for a bracelet. The shopkeeper can do nothing to enforce payment, since the minor no longer has the goods.

True / False ?

④ A minor can always drop out of a lease agreement, up to, and a short time after his 18th birthday.

True / False ?

⑤ A minor refuses to pay for a £50 coat delivered to his wife. The contract will be unenforceable since the coat was not for his personal use.

True / False ?

⑥ An adult guarantees a £300 loan to a minor. Both of them can refuse to repay it, if it is spent on non-necessaries.

True / False ?

CHAPTER FIVE - FORM OF A CONTRACT

Not all contracts have to be written.
Most can be made orally, even if it
involves large amounts of money.

However, some types of agreement must be in a certain form to be enforced:

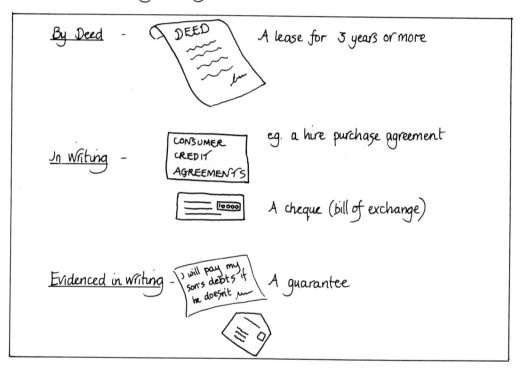

By Deed - *DEED*   A lease for 3 years or more

In Writing - *CONSUMER CREDIT AGREEMENTS*   eg. a hire purchase agreement

A cheque (bill of exchange)

Evidenced in writing - *I will pay my son's debts if he doesn't*   A guarantee

Signing a Contract

If a contract is written, the general rule is that you are bound by
all the terms, once you sign it.

But I didn't read all of it!

It's binding nonetheless

23

Terms of the Contract

When you make a contract, you agree
upon a number of things, not all of
which are vitally important to the contract

The time of arrival is vitally important, but the colour of the van is not.

Terms of a contract are divided into

- CONDITIONS (very important)
- WARRANTIES (not-so-important)
- INNOMINATE TERMS (in-between)

Conditions are terms which are vitally important to the contract

eg. | The tenant will pay rent promptly | or | The goods must be delivered by 9 am |

 If I breach a condition, the other party can sue me for damages and break off the contract altogether.

Warranties are terms which are of secondary importance and wouldn't ruin the whole contract if breached.

 If I breach a warranty, the other party can sue me for damages, but they can't break off the contract.

Innominate terms are terms where the courts look at how serious the effect of the breach was, and then classify them as conditions or warranties.

Terms and Representations

Not everything the seller says before the contract is made will be considered a term of the contract...

Written Contracts

If the contract is written down, anything said beforehand will not be a term of the contract unless it's included in the written agreement

This is called the Parol evidence rule

Unwritten Contracts

If the contract is not later written down, what is said in the negotiations may be a term of the contract, or a representation.

If it's a term, breach of it may release me from the contract, and allow me to claim damages from the person breaching it.

BUT

If it's a representation, and untrue, my remedy is an action for misrepresentation.

The test for whether a statement will be a term of the contract, or a representation is as follows...

① Reliance on the statement

"Take it from me, the horse is perfectly sound."

Schawel v. Reade 1913

Because the seller gave his assurance the horse was fine, and there was no need to check it, the statement was a term.

It would have been a representation if he'd told the buyer not to rely on it, but to examine the horse himself.

② If the truth of the statement was crucial to the person making the contract, it will probably be considered a term

I wouldn't have made the contract otherwise!

③ If the person making the statement has a special skill or knowledge about the subject, which the buyer relies upon, the statement is likely to be a term of the contract.

The car's done 20,000 miles

It had in fact done many more. The defendants were in a better position to know the mileage since they were car dealers, and the defendant wasn't. The statement was a term of the contract

Dick Bentley Productions, Ltd. v Harold Smith (motors), Ltd

QUIZ - FORM OF A CONTRACT

(1) "What is your trouble ? Is it grey hair? In ten days not a grey hair left - £500 Guarantee"
This type of statement would be regarded as mere trade puff, and no binding contractual terms would arise from it.

True/False ?

(2) A representation is a part of the contract, as a term.

True/False ?

(3) "This car's in great shape, take my word for it."
This statement would be a representation.

True/False?

(4) If the parties state something to be a condition of the contract, the courts will treat it as a condition, even if the result of the breach is very trivial.

True/False ?

(5) If a term in the contract is breached, there is an automatic right to damages.

True/False ?

Sometimes, even though the parties haven't expressly mentioned something as a term of the contract, it will be implied into the contract

> for example, if I buy a new pair of shoes, which then fall apart, this is a breach of condition by the seller.

The seller may not have stated anywhere that the shoes are in good condition, but the term is implied into the contract by the Sale of Goods Act 1979

Examples of implied terms

— the goods are of satisfactory quality

— if no price is mentioned beforehand, a reasonable price will be paid

When you ask for goods for a specific purpose, they'll be suitable for that purpose.

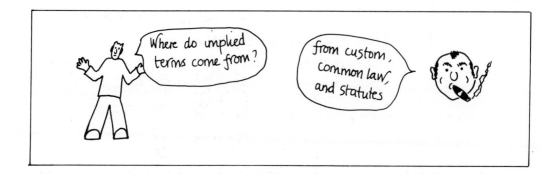

> Where do implied terms come from?

> from custom, common law, and statutes

<u>Terms implied by Custom</u>

This is the way it's done in the trade, everyone knows that

If this is the case, the trade practice, or custom, will be implied into the contract

---

<u>Terms implied by Common Law</u>

The courts will imply a term into a contract if it's obvious and necessary.

Lord Simon →

For a term to be implied... it must be so obvious that "it goes without saying"

For example, if you rent a room at the top of a house, it goes without saying that you can walk through the house to reach it

---

<u>Terms implied into certain contracts</u> (tenancy agreements, employment contracts)

e.g.
Tenancy Agreement

The contract will probably not state that house is fit for human habitation, but it's an implied term that it is

Another term implied by law, is that the landlord will leave the tenant in peace

Just come to join you for supper

Terms Implied By Statute

When you buy something from a shop, certain conditions are implied into the contract by The Sale of Goods Act 1979

for example ...   that the goods are of satisfactory quality (s. 14 (2))

that they belong to the person selling them (s.12)

that they fit their description (s. 13(1))

You said it was shrinkproof!

and that they're fit for the purpose they're sold for. (s. 14 (3))

These may not be stated anywhere, but the buyer can rely on them

So if the seller breaks any of the above conditions, I can get my money back!

Other statutes imply terms into a contract. For example - The Supply of Goods and Services Act 1982

This act applies to anyone giving a service, such as a bank
a builder
a plumber

It's implied into the contract that...

- The service will be carried out within a reasonable time (s. 14 (1))

- If no price is mentioned, a reasonable price will be paid (s. 15 (1))

 What happens if the contract the parties make is vague, or incomplete, can the courts still enforce it ?

 Examples of vague or incomplete contracts . . .

- Where the sale is on hire purchase terms with no description of what these are.

- Where no price is mentioned £—

- Where usual terms apply, and the parties have never contracted before

The courts have a number of methods to deal with vague or incomplete contracts

The court may
- Try to decide what the phrase means, by looking at trade custom
- Cut the confusing phrase out altogether
- or interpret it in a reasonable way

If the agreement is incomplete, certain terms can be implied by statute

 But no price is mentioned

The Sale of Goods Act, s. 8 states that a reasonable price is to be paid.

QUIZ - IMPLIED TERMS

① The implied term that goods will be of satisfactory quality does not apply to secondhand goods.

True / False ?

② If you buy an umbrella with a hole in it, which the shop assistant pointed out to you, you will later be able to return it, since it wasn't of satisfactory quality.

True / False ?

③ If an electrician comes to repair a fault on your television, but fails to find out what's wrong with it, you can refuse to pay him anything.

True / False ?

④ You buy some cloth described as 100% silk, and cut it up to make a shirt. You later realise it is only 75% silk, but it is too late to reject it at this point.

True / False ?

⑤ If you buy a piece of DIY equipment, described as 84cm long, and when you measure it, it is 84 ¼ cm long, will you be able to reject it, for not fitting the description, even though it is a very slight difference ?

Yes / No ?

CHAPTER SEVEN - EXCLUSION CLAUSES

Sometimes, one party may try to limit their liability by putting an exclusion (or exemption) clause in the contract

Examples of exclusion clauses are

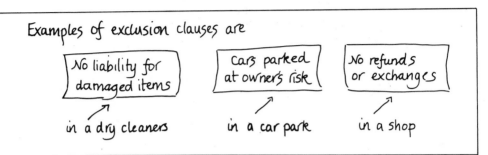

No liability for damaged items	Cars parked at owner's risk	No refunds or exchanges
in a dry cleaners	in a car park	in a shop

Some exclusion clauses are unfair .
They are controlled in two ways

— By the courts
— By statute

Control by the Courts

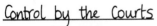

"To be effective, the exclusion clause must be written into the contract. If it isn't, we won't allow it."

TERMS — exclusion clause

The exclusion clause must be printed legibly and clearly

The more harsh, or unusual it is, the more clearly it must be pointed out to the person signing it. As Lord Denning said of one

"it would need to be printed in red ink, with a red hand pointing to it, or something equally startling."

The victim must be aware of the exclusion clause at the time the contract is made

there, now that's all signed, let me tell you about one or two hidden snags...

To mention the exclusion clause after the contract is made is too late.

The exclusion clause will not be allowed

If you sign a document, the usual rule is that you are bound by everything in it. However, in the following case, the plaintiff gave a wedding dress to be dry cleaned, and was asked to sign a form with an exclusion clause...

We are not liable for any damage to items left.

sign here _____

When she asked what exactly this meant, the defendants explained

Oh, that just means we're not liable for damage to beads and sequins on the dress

wrong information

The dress came back stained, and the dry cleaners were not allowed to rely on the exclusion clause, since they'd given her the wrong information at the time she signed it.

Curtis v Chemical Cleaning and Dyeing Co. 1951

If an oral promise is given at the time the contract is made, this will override a written exclusion clause.

Don't worry, your goods won't be carried on deck.

They were, and later...

Whoops!

GOODS

The defendants tried to rely on an exclusion clause in the written contract

No liability for damage to goods carried on deck

Your oral promise to the plaintiff means you cannot now rely on the written exclusion clause.

J. Evans & Son (Portsmouth) v. Andrea Merzario 1976

Another limitation on exclusion clauses is the

Contra Proferentem Rule

This means that if the meaning of the exclusion clause is unclear, we will interpret it against the party who wants to rely on it.

How are exclusion clauses controlled by statute ?

The Unfair Contract Terms Act 1977

No Liability for death or injury

This type of exclusion clause avoiding liability for death or injury caused by negligence will be completely void

s.2(1)

No responsibility for lost or damaged articles.

This exclusion clause will be allowed as long as it's reasonable

s.2(2)

NO REFUNDS OR EXCHANGES

This type of exclusion clause will not usually be allowed under the Unfair Contract Terms Act.

J'm a consumer, and you can't exclude any rights which are implied under the Sale of Goods Act. J can always get a refund if the goods are faulty, or don't match the description.

s. 6(2)

Jf it's a contract between two businesses, this type of exclusion clause may be allowed if it's reasonable

s. 6(3)

How do I know who is a business or a consumer ?

If you buy something from a shop or business, for your own personal use, you are a consumer

53 IBM computers, please

If the goods are not ordinarily for personal use, or are for business use, then your rights under the Sale of goods Act may be excluded if it's reasonable to do so.

Unfair Contract Terms Act, s. 11

The Test of Reasonableness

We decide if an exclusion clause is reasonable or not

The court looks at...

The bargaining power of the parties

Whether it was fair and reasonable to include the exclusion clause

Whether the party relying on the exclusion clause could have insured against the loss he's trying to avoid liability for.

s. 11

QUIZ - EXCLUSION CLAUSES

① A woman booked into a hotel, and on the back of her room door was a notice : "No liability for lost or stolen articles". Her fur coat was stolen from her room, but the hotel was not liable because of the exclusion clause.

True / False ?

② Once you sign a document with an exclusion clause, you will be bound by it.

True / False ?

③ "All rights under the Sale of Goods Act 1979 are excluded" This exclusion clause will be allowed if the contract is between two businesses

True / False ?

④ A man sitting in a deckchair was injured when it collapsed. On the back of the small deckchair ticket, was an exclusion clause : "No liability for injury". This exclusion clause was declared void since a deckchair ticket was not the place you would expect to find contractual conditions.

True / False ?

⑤ A sign in a shop saying "No Cash Refunds" would be a criminal offence, as well as void.

True / False ?

CHAPTER EIGHT · MISREPRESENTATION

A representation is not a binding contractual term. It is a statement made in the negotiations leading up to the contract

If the statement is untrue, it will be a misrepresentation, and can result in the contract being cancelled, or a claim for compensation.

The following rules apply for a statement to be a misrepresentation

The statement must have acted as an incentive for the other person to enter into the contract...

If it made no difference to the buyer whether it was true or not, they can't later claim for misrepresentation if it turns out to be untrue.

The statement will not be a misrepresentation usually, if it concerns future intention, or law.

Everyone is presumed to know the law

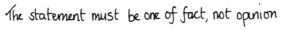

The statement must be one of fact, not opinion

In my opinion, this land could hold 2,000 sheep

It turned out that this was not true. It was not a misrepresentation, however, since he was stating an opinion, not a fact, and the land had never held sheep before.

<u>Bissett v. Wilkinson 1927</u>

The property is let to a most desirable tenant

It would be different, however, if the statement was something which the maker knew to be untrue,

This statement was a misrepresentation, even though it was expressed as an opinion, since the vendor knew it to be untrue

<u>Smith v Land and House Property Corporation 1885</u>

'Sales talk' will not usually amount to misrepresentation

for example  It goes like a bomb! Would be considered mere puff

but  It goes well over 200 mph. Would be a misrepresentation if untrue.

This is because the second is stating a specific fact.

Silence as misrepresentation

Usually, there must be a statement for there to be a misrepresentation. In some situations, though, silence can amount to a misrepresentation.

For example,

<u>If there is a change of circumstances</u>

 This doctor's practice makes £2,000 a year

This statement was true at the time, but when the contract was signed 5 months later, the takings had gone down to almost nothing, but the vendor didn't mention this.

Staying silent, when the circumstances had changed, would amount to misrepresentation

<u>With v. O'Flanagan 1936</u>

<u>Saying something which amounts to a half-truth</u>

 All the farms are let

This was true, but he didn't mention that all the tenants were about to leave.

By stating only half the facts, he gave a misleading picture, and this was held to be a misrepresentation.

<u>Dimmock v. Hallett 1866</u>

Contracts of Uberrima fides

In some types of contract, there is a duty to disclose all information, and not mentioning something could amount to misrepresentation

These types of contract are ones which require uberrima fides - the utmost good faith - for example insurance contracts

Generally, though there is no duty to disclose all the facts in most types of contract, but once you say something, it must be correct.

Certain types of behaviour may also be misleading. As Campbell L.C. remarked...

could constitute misleading behaviour, and the courts may refuse to enforce the contract because of this

> What remedy can I get, if I was misled into making the contract?

It depends on what type of misrepresentation it is....

INNOCENT misrepresentation

> But I thought it was true!

If the defendant wasn't careless in making the statement, the court may rescind (cancel) the contract, or if this is too drastic it may give damages instead.

NEGLIGENT misrepresentation

> I didn't check if it was true, and I had no reasonable grounds for believing it was true.

The court may rescind the contract, give damages, or give both remedies.

It's easier for the plaintiff to sue under the Misrepresentation Act 1967

(Then it's up to the defendant to prove it was reasonable for him to make the statement)

FRAUDULENT misrepresentation

> I made a statement which I knew was false, or in any case which I didn't care if it was true or not.

The plaintiff may ask the court to rescind the contract, and may claim damages either in contract or for the tort of deceit.

QUIZ · MISREPRESENTATION

① If you discover a painting you bought 5 years ago, is not
an original as you had been told, you will be able to rescind
(cancel) the contract.

True / False ?

② A tells B the car he's selling has done less than 15,000 miles.
B is a car dealer, who knows this to be untrue, but decides
to buy it anyway, then bring an action against A for
misrepresentation. Will this be possible ?

Yes / No ?

③ A car dealer tells the buyer that the car was once owned
by Nigel Mansell. The buyer shrugs, and says it makes
no difference. This will still be an actionable misrepresentation
if it turns out to be untrue.

True / False ?

④ In an application for a job as a travelling salesperson,
the successful applicant had not disclosed the fact that
they were disqualified from driving a car. Would silence
in these circumstances amount to a misrepresentation?

Yes / No ?

CHAPTER NINE - MISTAKE

A mistake can be
- mutual
- unilateral
- common

Mutual Mistake

To reach a valid agreement, there must be consensus ad idem

a meeting of minds

I'll sell you my car for £1,000

It's a deal

In this case both parties are at cross-purposes, there is no meeting of minds, and therefore no contract. Neither side can enforce the deal.

Unilateral Mistake

This occurs when only one party makes a mistake...

The plaintiff was negotiating to buy a house, and offered £2,000

The defendant replied... I will sell it for £1,250   He meant to say £2,250 and the plaintiff realised this.

I accept your offer   but I made a mistake!

The courts refused to enforce the deal.

Webster v. Cecil 1861

Common Mistake

This occurs where both parties make the same mistake.

e.g. a couple had just signed up a deed of separation, when they realised something important...

> We weren't lawfully married in the first place!

The separation agreement was void, because of this fundamental, common mistake.   <u>Galloway v. Galloway 1914</u>

A common mistake can also be where both parties agree to transfer property which (unknown to them) didn't exist, or had been destroyed.

A contract will not always be void for common mistake. For example...

> We both thought the painting was by John Constable, but it isn't.

<u>Leaf v. International Galleries 1950</u>

This is a common mistake as to the quality of the subject matter, rather than the existence of it, and cannot be void for mistake.

> an action may lie for misrepresentation, or breach of contract

Mistake as to Identity

This occurs when you make a contract with someone, believing them to be someone else...

 My name's P.G.M. Hutchinson. Here's a cheque for your car - Can J drive it away now?

 Oh yes, here you are in the phone book.

The man was an impostor and the cheque turned out to be worthless. By the time they discovered this, he'd sold the car to someone else.

 Can we have our car back, please?

Yes, the contract was void, because you never meant to contract with that rogue.

Ingram v. Little 1960

This view changed in a later case, where a similar situation arose...

impostor

 He said he was an actor, and showed me his studio pass. The cheque he gave me for the car is worthless, but he's already sold it to someone else.

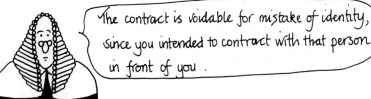 The contract is voidable for mistake of identity, since you intended to contract with that person in front of you.

The third party kept the car, since he bought it <u>before</u> the contract was avoided.

Lewis v. Averay 1972

47

Non est factum

Another type of mistake concerns documents...

> Please sign these top secret documents without reading them. We need your signature as a witness.

The defendant signed the documents, which in fact were two promissory notes.

> You can plead non est factum – 'not my deed', and the contract will be void for mistake.

Lewis v. Clay 1897

To plead non est factum you must show...

- The signature was induced by fraud
- The document was fundamentally different from what it was thought to be.
- The party pleading non est factum was not negligent

> I signed a document which I thought transferred my house to my nephew, but I couldn't read it because my glasses were broken.

The document in fact transferred the house to someone else, and the widow pleaded non est factum.

> The plea cannot be available to anyone who was content to sign without taking the trouble to find out at least the general effect of the document.

Saunders v. Anglia Building Society Ltd. 1971

48

QUIZ - MISTAKE

① B signed a promissory note, believing it to be for £100.
In fact he had been tricked, through no fault of his own,
and it was in fact for £1,000.
Will B be able to plead non est factum?

Yes / No ?

② If you make a contract with someone, believing them to
be something they are not (very rich, for example) the
contract will be voidable for mistake, if they tricked you
into believing this.

True / False ?

③ A man signed a bank form, the contents of which were not
properly explained to him by the bank. He was, in fact,
illiterate, but he didn't mention this. Could he plead
non est factum?

Yes / No ?

④ A buys a car from B, under an assumed name. By the
time B realises the cheque A gave him is worthless, A
has already sold the car. B will be able to reclaim the car.

True / False ?

⑤ A mistake will always render the contract void.

True / False ?

Contracts made under duress

sign this, or else...

If someone is forced into signing a contract, it will not bind them later, since it was made under duress.

Examples of duress include   – a threat to physically harm someone, or their close family

– a threat of dishonour

but not a threat to harm goods

A threat of unlawful imprisonment can also count as duress...

If you don't sign over your property, we'll put you in a mental home!

Since she'd agreed under duress, the agreement was not binding

Cumming v. Ince 1847

What happens if J was forced into making the contract?

Contracts made under duress are voidable. That means you can choose to avoid it, if you dont want to go on with it.

Undue Influence

Whereas duress is forcing someone to make a contract, undue influence involves pressurizing or influencing someone in such a way, that they don't make a free choice

Relationships where undue influence is presumed are...

solicitor and client

doctor and patient

parent and child

religious adviser and disciple

The presumption of undue influence is rebuttable, so it's up to me to prove I didn't unfairly influence the weaker party.

Undue Influence can be of many types. Lord Denning defined it in terms of inequality of bargaining power where...

The parties have not met on equal terms ...it is not right that the strong should be allowed to push the weak to the wall.

Lloyds Bank v. Bundy 1975

51

For a claim of undue influence to be successful, the contract must clearly be to the weaker party's disadvantage.

> I signed without fully understanding the facts, and without having independent legal advice

If undue influence is proved, the contract is voidable, and the party may apply to the court to have it set aside.

> We will do so, if it's fair

To rescind (cancel) the contract, however, it must be done within a reasonable time...

> When I left the religious order, I'd given them a large amount of my property. Now I want it back.

> But you left the order six years ago! You should have brought your claim to court before then, or we'll assume that you agreed to go on with the contract.

Allcard v. Skinner 1887

QUIZ - DURESS AND UNDUE INFLUENCE

① The relationship of husband and wife is one where undue influence is automatically presumed.

True / False ?

② A threat to burn your house down can constitute duress.

True / False ?

③ A threat to take someone to court for money owed, can constitute duress, if you knew the result would bankrupt that person.

True / False ?

④ A wife was pressurized by her husband into signing a mortgage deed for their property. This was done in order to save their business. Would she be able to have the charge set aside for undue influence?

Yes / No ?

⑤ A father signed a mortgage form giving a charge over his property to the bank. This was to prevent the bank from prosecuting his son for forging promissory notes. The father was not able to set this charge aside since it was to his advantage.

True / False ?

CHAPTER ELEVEN - ILLEGALITY

£10,000 if you get rid of my husband.

OK

A contract to do something illegal will not be enforced by the courts.

This principle is called 'Ex turpi causa non oritur actio' and means that no action can be brought on an illegal act

Romer L.J. →

an agreement to do an act that is illegal or immoral or contrary to public policy... is unlawful and therefore void.

A contract will be illegal if it involves breaking a law, either at the outset, or after the contract is formed.

In 1725, two highwaymen robbed a coach...

But we agreed to share the loot!

You can't sue me for it, the agreement was illegal.

Everet v Williams 1725

This includes both criminal and civil laws, for example, a contract to publish something libellous would be illegal, since this is a tort · a civil wrong.

Other types of illegal contracts include

- Contracts which encourage sexual immorality (Pearce v Brooks 1866)

- Contracts which are contrary to public policy (eg. allowing someone to profit from a crime)

- Contracts which interfere with the course of justice (eg. an agreement to stifle a criminal prosecution)

- Contracts to defraud the inland revenue

What happens if the agreement is illegal?

The contract will be void and unenforceable, and any money or property transferred will be lost, and not recoverable.

The situation is different if the contract is legal at the outset, but one party then uses it for illegal purposes.

If J didn't know about the illegal purpose, J can recover any money or property transferred.

(eg. hiring a room to give blasphemous lectures - Cowan v. Milbourn 1867)

Contracts in Restraint of Trade

EMPLOYMENT CONTRACT
J will not carry on a similar trade when J leave, within 500 miles of this area.

Contracts which stop someone from carrying on a trade or profession are prima facie void as they are against public policy.

Employers may try to protect their business interest by putting a clause in the contract, forbidding the employee to compete within a certain area, or to give away trade secrets. These restraints are allowed if reasonable...

eg. to protect business connections

But he's taking all my customers away!

If this was a possibility the restraint might be held to be reasonable

However, even if the restraint is allowed, it must be for a reasonable time, and within a reasonable area.

He agreed not to canvass within 25 miles of London!

← ex-employee

But that area is 1,000 times bigger than the area he worked for you in. The restraint is unreasonable!

<u>Mason v. Provident Clothing Co. Ltd 1913</u>

What is reasonable will depend on the type of contract and the circumstances.

QUIZ - ILLEGALITY

① The plaintiff hired out a carriage to a prostitute, knowing she would use it to carry out her trade. When she fell behind with the payments, he could enforce payment since his particular agreement was not illegal.

True /False ?

② A contract not to sue someone for a civil wrong will be illegal.

True /False ?

③ A contract where one party voluntarily promises not to marry will be void.

True /False ?

④ A lifelong ban on an employee working as a solicitor within seven miles of the area would be unreasonable, even though a solicitor keeps clients for many years.

True /False ?

⑤ A husband and wife make a contract concerning any possible future separation. This contract would be void as it is against public policy.

True /False ?

CHAPTER TWELVE - DISCHARGE OF A CONTRACT

 (How does a contract come to an end ?)

There are four ways
a contract is discharged
- Performance
- Agreement
- Breach
- Frustration

Performance

The usual rule is that a contract is discharged when it's performed exactly according to the terms of the contract. Anything less will not do.

This is called the rule in <u>Cutter v. Powell 1795</u>

(I'm working on this ship from Jamaica to England, for thirty guineas.)

When the ship was over halfway there, he died, and his widow sued for payment for the part of the journey he'd already done, on a quantum meruit basis (as much as he earned)

(Part payment will not be made.
The contract was to do the whole journey,
and it was not completed.)

The difference can be minimal ...

 order form
for tins of fruit
in boxes of 30 tins

When the goods arrived, the buyer rejected them

 But we sent you the right number of tins!

 But some of them are in boxes of 24, not 30

Since it was a sale by description, the goods must strictly match the description. They didn't, so performance wasn't complete. The buyer could reject the goods, and refuse to pay for them.

Re Moore & Co. Ltd. and Landauer & Co's Arbitration 1921

So I didn't do it correctly, can I claim for what I did?

Unless it is a divisible contract, the plaintiff cannot claim on a 'quantum meruit' basis...

 I fitted central heating for the defendant, and now he won't pay!

 That's because it doesn't work!

The plaintiff could not recover any of the money he claimed.

Bolton v. Mahadeva 1972

Are there any exceptions to the rule that performance must be complete?

Severable or Divisible Contracts

These are contracts which can be divided into parts, or are payable in instalments

I can claim payment as I finish each part

Fault of the Other Party

I don't want it anymore

If you make it impossible for the other party to finish the contract, they can claim for payment on a quantum meruit basis, or sue for breach of contract.

Substantial Performance

You missed a bit. I'm not paying.

If there are just a few minor defects, the decorator can claim the contract price, minus the costs of putting it right. (Hoenig v. Isaac 1952)

However, if it costs any more than ¼ of the contract price to put right the defects, this would probably not count as substantial performance.

When the other party accepts partial performance

Ok, you've done most of it, I'll pay you for what you've done

Agreement

The parties can also end the contract by mutual agreement.

I'll give up my rights to enforce the contract

and I'll give up mine.

When neither side has performed his part of the contract, then both sides give consideration by the promise not to enforce the contract.

However, if one side has already performed their part of the contract, they cannot release the other from their obligation, without some consideration from them (eg. payment of a cancellation fee.)

This is because of the rule in Pinnel's case.

If the other party gives no consideration for the new agreement, there's nothing to stop me going back on the agreement.

Promissory Estoppel may work, however, to prevent that person from going back on their promise.

Breach

The contract may end when one of the parties breaches the agreement

The breach may be an actual breach...

> I'm sorry, your goods won't be ready on time

or an anticipatory breach...

> I'm telling you in advance, I'm breaking off the agreement

NB
An actual breach can also occur when one party doesn't carry out the contract properly.

The effect of the breach depends on whether it is a fundamental breach, breach of a condition, or of a warranty...

innocent party

> I will be able to sue for damages, and if it's a very serious breach, I can treat myself as no longer having to go on with the contract.

So if the contract was for delivery of goods at a certain time, and they arrive late, the buyer can sue for damages, and may be able to refuse to accept the goods.

Discharge of a contract by Frustration

 If something happens without fault of either party, to make performance impossible, illegal, or radically different, both parties are excused from the contract.

For example...

 I hired a music hall for a day, and it burnt down beforehand. Am I still bound to pay under the contract?

No. Destruction of the subject-matter means the contract is frustrated.

Taylor v. Caldwell 1863

On non-occurrence of an event...

 I hired a room just to watch the King's coronation, which was cancelled. Do I still have to take the room?

No, since that was the only reason you took the room, the contract is frustrated.

Krell v. Henry 1903

(If he'd had another purpose for renting the room, the contract would not have been frustrated)

If the contract is frustrated, the Law Reform (Frustrated Contracts) Act 1934 applies

This means any money paid is recoverable, and any money payable ceases to be payable.

Times when frustration will not apply

Self-induced frustration

If I'm responsible for the event which makes performance impossible, I cannot claim frustration, and I may be sued for breach of contract.

When one party gives an absolute undertaking to perform

I will carry out the contract, whatever happens

Onerous Contracts

Since we agreed to this contract, the price of labour has gone up, and so has the cost of performing it. Can we claim frustration?

No. Inflation or labour shortage will not amount to frustration.

Davis Contractors Ltd. v. Fareham U.D.C. 1956

Events expressly provided for in the contract

In the event of war/strikes etc..

Often known as a 'hardship clause' this may cancel the contract, or suspend it for a while.

QUIZ - DISCHARGE

① A trader orders 25 boxes of goods, and 26 are delivered. He will be able to reject all the goods, even though he could easily leave the one extra box.

True / False ?

② The defendant hired a boat to watch the naval review, and cruise around the fleet. The naval review was cancelled. Was the contract frustrated?

Yes / No ?

③ A builder agrees to erect a certain number of buildings. When he's halfway through, he runs out of money and has to stop. Could he claim payment for what he's already done, since he was prevented from finishing them?

Yes / No ?

④ A agrees to hire a hall out to B for New Year's Eve, and then three weeks before that date, A announces that he's breaking off the agreement. B says nothing, and the next week the hall is destroyed by fire. Can B still bring an action against A for breach of contract?

Yes / No ?

CHAPTER THIRTEEN - REMEDIES

When a term of a contract is breached, various remedies are available

- Damages
- Injunction
- Specific Performance
- Rescission
- Rectification

Damages

The aim of damages is to put the injured party in the same financial position he would have been in, if the contract was properly carried out

However, not all loss will be recoverable ...

You took so long to bring back the mill shaft, our mill's been out of action for a week!

How could we know this?

The defendants had no idea the mill would be out of action - so the plaintiffs couldn't claim for the resulting loss of profit

<u>Hadley v. Baxendale 1854</u>

To be able to claim for damages, the loss must be something which is a natural consequence of the breach, or which both parties contemplated might happen, at the time they made the contract.

If I envisaged a particular type of loss, it will make no difference if the extent of it is then much greater than I imagined.

The amount of damages may be liquidated

ie.

Fixed in the contract
Damages for breach,
£2,000

or unliquidated

So we must decide
how much to award

If the amount of liquidated damages is much higher than the actual loss suffered, it may be considered a penalty clause, which can be struck out by the courts, and a fairer amount substituted.

Duty to mitigate the loss

I must keep my losses to a minimum, or I may not be able to claim all of them in damages.

Damages for refusal to accept goods

He agreed to buy my car, and now he doesn't want it!

If the seller can sell the goods immediately to another person, for the same price, he's suffered no loss.

If, however, he gets a lower price, he can claim the difference in damages.

<u>Injunction</u>

An injunction is a court order, stopping a person from doing something which breaches a term in the agreement....

CONTRACT
I will not work for anyone else for 1 year.
<u>Bette Davis</u>

The actress did try to work for another film company, and an injunction was granted.

This stopped me from working for anyone else.

<u>Warner Bros. Pictures Inc. v. Nelson 1937</u>

<u>Specific Performance</u>

This is a court order which makes the defendant carry out their promise under the contract

He agreed to sell me his Vintage Rolls Royce!

An order of specific performance would compel the defendant to sell the car as agreed.

We'll give an order of specific performance when damages aren't enough to compensate.

However, specific performance will not be granted to enforce a contract for personal services such as teaching, or an agreement to work for someone.

NB
Both these remedies are discretionary

So we'll only grant them when it's fair.

QUIZ - REMEDIES

① A breaks a contract he made with B, to pay C £100.
Can C enforce the contract against A ?

Yes / No ?

② A breach of contract meant the plaintiff had to live
with his in-laws. Would he be able to claim damages
for physical inconvenience ?

Yes / No ?

③ The defendant wrongly refused to accept a horse he'd
contracted to buy. The plaintiff had to keep it for a
year until he could find another buyer, who paid much
less than the defendant had agreed to pay.
Would the plaintiff be able to claim the expenses of
keeping the horse for a year, as well as the loss of
profit, in damages ?

Yes / No ?

④ A has contracted to deliver a car to B in July.
In May, he announces that he will not be delivering
the car. A cannot bring an action for breach
until July.

True / False ?

⑤ A minor will be granted the remedy of specific performance.

True / False ?

QUIZ ANSWERS

Chapter One - Offer and Acceptance

① No — You can't claim a reward when you didn't know of the offer (Fitch v. Snedaker 1868)

② No — Acceptance of a unilateral contract need not be communicated, and if a letter of acceptance is posted it may not arrive, but there may still be a binding contract.

③ Yes — As long as they didn't give any consideration to keep the offer open (eg a deposit)

④ No — this is because the postman was delivering letters. (Re London and Northern Bank 1900)

⑤ True — This was not a counter offer, since it was phrased as a question.

⑥ False — It would be a valid acceptance as long as it was by a method which was equally fast.

Chapter Two - Consideration

① No — Their consideration is past

② Yes — A trivial act can be consideration, it need not be adequate (Gilbert v. Ruddeard 1608)

③ False — He can, as long as he gives you reasonable notice. He cannot, however, claim payment of arrears of rent.

④ No — Only someone who's given consideration can enforce a promise (Tweddle v. Atkinson 1861)

⑤ False — Their act was done in return for your promise.

⑥ False — It will be enforceable if it's made by deed.

QUIZ ANSWERS

Chapter Three - Intention to Create Legal Relations

① No   It was a social arrangement, with no intention to create legal relations.

② Yes   On the authority of Simpkins v. Pays 1955 the prize money would have to be shared out as agreed.

③ True   In Jones v. Vernons Pools 1938 these words meant that the contract was not legally binding.

④ False   It may be binding, as in Synge v. Synge 1894, especially if that party gives up their accommodation in return.

⑤ True   An agreement between a family was binding in the case Snelling v. John G. Snelling Ltd. 1973

Chapter Four - Capacity To Contract

① False   This does not apply if the minor has already paid for goods.

② False   He can recover a reasonable price, not necessarily the price he is asking.

③ False   The court may order the minor to hand over that item instead.

④ True

⑤ False   A contract for necessaries for the minor's wife (or children) will be enforceable

⑥ False   The Minor's Contracts Act 1987 means that an adult guaranteeing a loan made to a minor will be obliged to repay it.

QUIZ ANSWERS

Chapter Five - Form of a Contract

① False   In Wood v. Lectrik Ltd 1932, this advert was held to have binding contractual effect.

② False   A representation is a statement made in negotiations which induces the contract.

③ False   It's likely to be a term, since the party making it is assuring the other of its truth.

④ False   In exceptional circumstances, the courts will disregard what the parties said, and refuse to treat something as a condition if it's something very trivial, but will treat it instead as a warranty.
(L. Schuler AG v. Wickham Machine Tool Sales 1973)

⑤ True   There is no automatic right to damages, however, if a representation turns out to be untrue.

Chapter Six - Implied Terms

① False   It will still apply, but a lower standard is acceptable.

② False   You will not be able to, if the defect was pointed out beforehand.

③ True   But only if he's failed to spot an obvious defect.

④ True   You can reject goods until you have accepted them. This means doing anything inconsistent with the rights of the seller (e.g. cutting it up) - The Sale of Goods Act 1979, s. 35

⑤ True   The difference can be minimal.
(Moore & Co. v. Landauer & Co. 1921)

QUIZ ANSWERS

Chapter Seven - Exclusion Clauses

① False   The contract was made at the reception area, she didn't see the exclusion clause until she reached her room, so it wasn't part of the contract (<u>Olley v. Marlborough Court, Ltd 1949</u>)

② False   It may be void by statute, or misleading information may override it.

③ False   s.12 - The goods belong to the person selling them, can never be excluded.

④ True   <u>Chapelton v. Barry UDC 1940</u>. This type of exclusion clause would now be void under the Unfair Contract Terms Act 1977

⑤ True   Under the Fair Trading Act 1973, any trader who tries to make customers think their rights under the Sale of goods Act are excluded, will have committed a criminal offence.

Chapter Eight - Misrepresentation

① False   The right to rescind is lost after a reasonable time.

② No   There is no action for misrepresentation when the plaintiff knew the statement was untrue.

③ False   The statement must induce that person to make the contract.

④ No   There is only a duty to disclose information in contracts of the utmost good faith (insurance, or partnership contracts, etc.)

QUIZ ANSWERS

Chapter Nine - Mistake

① No — The document was not fundamentally different from what he believed it to be. It was still a promissory note.

② False — The contract will only be voidable for mistake if it concerns the actual identity of the person, not their personal attributes.

③ Yes — He was not negligent since he had enquired about the effect of the guarantee (Lloyds Bank v. Waterhouse 1990)

④ False — A has a voidable title and can sell the car to someone else, any time until B realises the mistake.

⑤ False

Chapter Ten - Duress and Undue Influence

① False — It is up to the party seeking to avoid the contract to show undue influence.

② True.

③ False — A threat to enforce your contractual rights is not illegal.

④ No — The contract must be shown to be to her manifest disadvantage, before it will be set aside.
(Midland Bank v. Shephard 1987)

⑤ False — The contract was void (Williams v. Bayley 1866)

QUIZ ANSWERS

Chapter Eleven – Illegality

① False   The contract would be void for immorality
      (Pearce v. Brooks 1866)

② False   This is only the case for a criminal wrong

③ True   It will be void since it is against public policy.

④ False   A lifelong restraint was allowed in the case
      Fitch v Dewes 1921. This was held to be reasonable
      since a solicitor may keep many clients for life

⑤ True   It would not be void, however, if it was regarding an
      immediate separation, or if they had just been
      reconciled after a previous separation.

Chapter Twelve – Discharge of a Contract

① True   This is because they do not correspond exactly
      with the terms of the contract, set out in
      section 30 (2), Sale of Goods Act 1979

② False   Watching the naval review was not the only reason
      for hiring the boat (Herne Bay Steamboat Co. v. Hutton 1903).

③ No   This happened in Sumpter v. Hedges 1898. The plaintiff
      was not allowed to claim on a quantum meruit basis,
      since the contract was not divisible, and had not
      been frustrated.

④ No   It was an anticipatory breach, and before B took
      action, the contract was frustrated.

QUIZ ANSWERS

Chapter Thirteen - Remedies

① No — C was not a party to the contract. Only someone who is a party to the contract can enforce it. This is referred to as privity of contract.

② Yes — This happened in _Bailey v Bullock 1950_

③ Yes — As long as he had acted reasonably in keeping the horse for so long before he sold it (_Hoffberger v Ascot International Bloodstock Bureau 1976_)

INDEX